PROSPERING BY FAITH & WISDOM

A KINGDOM ENTREPRENEUR'S GUIDE TO BUSINESS SUCCESS

OTESCIA R. JOHNSON

Copyright © 2025

PROPSERING BY FAITH & WISDOM: A Kingdom Entrepreneur's Guide to Business Success- Otescia R. Johnson

Please direct all copyright inquiries to:
orjohnson@alwaysbetonyourself.com

PAPERBACK ISBN: 978-1-955605-89-2

Cover and Interior Design - B.O.Y. Enterprises, Inc.

Printed in the United States of America

TABLE OF CONTENTS

CHAPTER

Discovering Your Purpose: Understanding Your Calling in Business

"For we are God's masterpiece. He has created us anew in Christ Jesus, so we can do the good things he planned for us long ago."
— Ephesians 2:10 (NLT)

Discovering Your Purpose: Understanding Your Calling in Business

Introduction: You Were Born for This

There's a stirring inside you that won't go away—a holy dissatisfaction with doing "just enough." You're not chasing fame, but you know you were made for something greater than a 9-to-5 existence. That's not arrogance. That's calling. That's purpose. And as a Kingdom entrepreneur, you have not only been saved by grace but also called to work that brings glory to God and impact to others.

Your business isn't just a way to pay the bills—it's a divine assignment. It's a response to the needs God allows you to see. Your unique experiences, skillsets, and passions are not random. They are ingredients in a purposeful design—a Kingdom blueprint. But before you start marketing strategies or building revenue streams, you must first understand what God has called you to do.

Purpose Is Revealed, Not Invented

In the world, people talk about "creating your purpose." But in the Kingdom, purpose is not self-made—it's God-given.

"The Lord has made everything for his own purposes..."
— Proverbs 16:4a (NLT)

You don't have to stumble in the dark or chase every opportunity hoping something works. You can seek the Lord, and He will reveal your assignment in due season. That's the difference between a good idea and a God idea. The world is full of talented people with clever business models. But Kingdom entrepreneurs are different—we move by revelation, not trend.

"Your own ears will hear him. Right behind you a voice will say, 'This is the way you should go,' whether to the right or to the left."

— Isaiah 30:21 (NLT)

Your Business Is a Ministry

You don't need a pulpit to do ministry. If your business brings solutions, promotes integrity, and blesses others, then your business is already a platform for purpose. Whether you're baking bread, styling hair, consulting clients, or teaching online courses—your excellence and faith are preaching louder than any sermon. You are God's ambassador in the marketplace. Remember, your business is God's response to someone else's prayer.

"Work willingly at whatever you do, as though you were working for the Lord rather than for people."

— Colossians 3:23 (NLT)

This mindset shift is critical. When you realize your business is a ministry:
- You stop comparing your journey to others.
- You become more focused on serving people, not selling to them.
- You find strength to keep going, even when the money isn't matching the mission...yet.

Purpose will always be connected to:

1. What breaks your heart
2. What fires you up
3. Who you feel called to help
4. Where you see a gap you know how to fill

God won't call you to everything—but He will call you to something specific.

Ask yourself:

- What injustices frustrate me?
- What comes naturally to me that others struggle with?
- What problem do I feel equipped to solve?
- Who am I uniquely positioned to serve?

"If you need wisdom, ask our generous God, and he will give it to you. He will not rebuke you for asking."

— James 1:5 (NLT)

Ask boldly. Listen humbly. And move obediently.

Don't Despise Small Beginnings

Purpose often starts small. You may begin with just an idea, a hobby, or one client. Don't let the size of your start discourage you.

"Do not despise these small beginnings, for the Lord rejoices to see the work begin..."

— Zechariah 4:10a (NLT)

God doesn't need you to be perfect; He needs you to be positioned. When you start walking in purpose—even if it's just one step—He'll order the rest.

Let God Define the Metrics

In business, the world teaches us to measure success through numbers—sales, followers, email subscribers, brand reach, and profit margins. But when you're building something for the Kingdom, God uses a different scoreboard.

He doesn't measure your worth or success by the size of your platform or the number of zeros in your revenue report. He measures your obedience, consistency, faithfulness, and heart posture. These are Heaven's KPIs—Kingdom Performance Indicators.

"People may be pure in their own eyes, but the Lord examines their motives." — **Proverbs 16:2 (NLT)**

That's why you can't compare your beginning to someone else's breakthrough. And you can't afford to let "likes" or "launch results" determine whether or not you're walking in your purpose. God cares more about the why than the wow.

The Widow's Oil (2 Kings 4:1–7)

Let's consider the story of the widow who came to the prophet Elisha in desperation. Her husband had died, and a creditor was threatening to take her two sons as payment. She had nothing—at least in her own eyes.

But Elisha asked her a pivotal question:
"Tell me, what do you have in the house?" — 2 Kings 4:2 (NLT)

Her reply? "Nothing at all, except a flask of olive oil," she replied.

That's where God began.

Elisha instructed her to borrow as many empty jars as she could from her neighbors. Then he told her to go inside, close the door, and pour the little oil she had into those jars. As she obeyed, the oil multiplied—but only as long as there were vessels available to receive it.

Once the last jar was filled, the oil stopped flowing. She was then able to sell the oil, pay her debts, and live off the rest.

This story shows us a divine principle:
➡ God doesn't need a lot to do a lot.
➡ He multiplies what you surrender, not what you impress people with.
➡ The metrics that matter most are your obedience and your capacity to follow instructions, not your visibility.

If the widow had only focused on how small her oil was, she would've missed her miracle. The oil wasn't the issue—her faith and obedience were the determining factors.

Are You Focused on Metrics or on Ministry?

If you're not careful, you'll think you're failing because your audience is small, your income isn't "six-figure" yet, or your growth seems slow. But ask yourself:
• Did I do what God told me to do?
• Am I showing up with excellence, even if no one is clapping yet?
• Is my heart still surrendered, or have I made success an idol?

"Seek the Kingdom of God above all else, and live righteously, and he will give you everything you need." — **Matthew 6:33 (NLT)**

Success in the Kingdom is tied to alignment, not applause. You can be building something small on earth but be considered great in Heaven because you're aligned, faithful, and obedient. So yes, track your growth. Set financial goals. Use wisdom. But never let numbers have the final say over your faith. God's favor can accomplish more in one act of obedience than years of human striving ever could

Reflection Prompt:

Take time to reflect and pray through the following:
- Am I letting comparison distort how I define success?
- Have I overlooked what's "in my house"—the skills, experiences, and tools God already gave me?
- Am I measuring obedience... or just output?

"And what do you benefit if you gain the whole world but lose your own soul?" — **Mark 8:36 (NLT)**

Let God define the metrics. Because when you follow His model, you don't just prosper—you prosper by faith.

Journal Pages
Chapter 1

Scripture to Meditate On

"Seek the Kingdom of God above all else, and live righteously, and he will give you everything you need." — **Matthew 6:33 (NLT)**

⊛ Self-Check: Am I Measuring the Right Things?

Circle one that applies to your current mindset:

I feel successful when...

- I'm being obedient to God
- I hit my financial goals
- Others validate my work
- I'm making consistent progress

What stood out to you from the story of the widow and the oil in 2 Kings 4:1–7?

_____

_____

_____

_____

_____

_____

_____

_____

_____

Journal Page
Chapter 1

Reflection Questions

1. What has God already placed "in your house" (skills, experiences, tools) that you've overlooked or underestimated?

_____

_____

_____

_____

2. What small act of obedience do you need to take this week, even if it doesn't seem "big enough" yet?

_____

_____

_____

_____

3. How have you allowed metrics (likes, sales, followers) to define your worth or progress? What truth can replace that mindset?

_____

_____

_____

_____

Prayer of Surrender

Heavenly Father,

I surrender my ideas of success and invite You to define the metrics of my life and business. Teach me to value obedience over outcomes. Help me to trust that what You've given me is enough, and that You are the God who multiplies what I place in Your hands. Remove every spirit of comparison and self-doubt. I declare that I will walk by faith, not by sight. In Jesus' name, amen.

Personal Notes or Prayers:

_____

_____

_____

_____

_____

_____

_____

_____

_____

_____

_____

_____

_____

CHAPTER 2

The Power of Prayer: Building a Strong Spiritual Foundation for Your Business

"Don't worry about anything; instead, pray about everything. Tell God what you need, and thank him for all he has done." **— Philippians 4:6 (NLT)**

The Power of Prayer: Building a Strong Spiritual Foundation for Your Business

Prayer is Your Strategy, Not a Last Resort

Every thriving business has a strategy—marketing plans, operational systems, financial models. But as a Kingdom entrepreneur, your greatest advantage isn't just what you know —it's Who you know. Communicating with God will always be the secret sauce to a Kingdom Entrepreneur's success. Prayer isn't just for Sundays or spiritual emergencies. It is the engine that drives every wise decision, divine connection, and supernatural breakthrough in your business. Without prayer, you're building on sand. With prayer, you're building on the Rock.

"Unless the Lord builds a house, the work of the builders is wasted." **— Psalm 127:1a (NLT)**

None of us have time to waste. Therefore, it is critical that you remember to allow God to build your business. God saw this day before the foundations of the world and made provision for it. He knew you'd be sitting in the exact spot you're sitting in reading this. He knew the earth would be ripe for what He has been building in you. And He knows exactly what you need to do to see every promise made manifest in your life. So before you draft the business plan or launch the next product—have you prayed?

Business Is Spiritual

Some entrepreneurs separate their faith from their business, operating like God cares about their soul but not their success. But everything in the Kingdom is spiritual—including your pricing, your proposals, and your purpose. I've done the testing and hard work for you, so let me save you some time and energy. God wants to be involved in every decision you make. From the brand colors you choose to the design and flow of your website.

God wants to be your:
- Chief Marketing Officer
- Boardroom Advisor
- Brand Manager
- Contract Negotiator
- Business Developer

He wants to be involved in every part of the process, from your launch date to your invoices. When you pray, you give Him access to do what only He can. Remember we know in part but when God looks at you and your business, He sees the beginning, middle, and end all in real time, AT THE SAME TIME! He knows how many customers are going to buy your next product, so before you start ordering supplies, pause and ask Him how many you should order!

"The Lord directs the steps of the godly. He delights in every detail of their lives."

— Psalm 37:23 (NLT)

Examples of Business Breakthroughs Through Prayer

Look at Nehemiah. He wasn't a prophet or a priest—he was a cupbearer with a burden to rebuild Jerusalem's walls. He was no different from me or you, just a servant of the Lord with a prayer burden given to him by God as a response to a need in the Earth. Before approaching the king for support, Nehemiah prayed and fasted.

"When I heard this, I sat down and wept. In fact, for days I mourned, fasted, and prayed to the God of heaven."
— Nehemiah 1:4 (NLT)

As a result, God gave him favor with the king, resources for the assignment, and protection during opposition. His work prospered because he prayed and obtained favor from God BEFORE he moved forward with his Earthly assignment.

And then there's Solomon. When given the opportunity to ask for anything, he chose wisdom to lead the people well. His request pleased God so much that He gave him wisdom, riches, and long life—all because Solomon made his first business move in prayer, and he asked for the most valuable asset any of us can ever ask for... wisdom!

"So give me the wisdom and knowledge to lead them properly..."
— 2 Chronicles 1:10 (NLT)

Solomon gained the wisdom he needed to lead the people because he prioritized his faith and asked God for wisdom. God does not show favoritism between His children. The same way He honored Solomon's faith and request, He will honor yours. Whether you are continuing in an industry you are familiar with or stepping into a completely new venture, prioritizing your faith and seeking the wisdom of God will always guide you towards success and open doors.

What Happens When You Prioritize Prayer in Business

As Kingdom entrepreneurs, we must recognize that prayer is not a religious ritual—it's a spiritual power source. It's how we partner with God in building something that's not only profitable but purposeful. When you put prayer first, it changes everything. Here's how:

1. You Gain Clarity

Prayer is the place where confusion dies and direction is born. In the stillness of God's presence, you can hear the whisper that cuts through noise, doubt, and overwhelm. How often do we jump from one idea to the next, chasing trends, algorithms, and opinions—yet never pause long enough to ask God, "What are You saying about this?" Prayer brings alignment. It exposes distractions and centers your focus on what truly matters.

"Your word is a lamp to guide my feet and a light for my path."

— Psalm 119:105 (NLT)

"The Lord says, 'I will guide you along the best pathway for your life. I will advise you and watch over you."

— Psalm 32:8 (NLT)

God's guidance isn't vague—it's specific, timely, and tailor-made for your journey. But you won't receive it without relationship. When you pray, you access divine clarity that cuts through chaos and confusion.

2. You Receive Divine Strategy

There are some ideas, downloads, and instructions that only come from prayer. These are not things you learn in a webinar or a mastermind— they are revealed in the secret place. Consider how God gave Joshua a military strategy to conquer Jericho that made no sense in the natural: walk around the city walls for six days, then shout on the seventh. That was a divine strategy—and it worked.

When you pray, you position yourself to receive Heaven's blueprints for your business.

"Call to me and I will answer you and tell you great and unsearchable things you do not know."

— Jeremiah 33:3 (NLT)

"It is God who arms me with strength and makes my way perfect. He makes me as surefooted as a deer, enabling me to stand on mountain heights. He trains my hands for battle..."

— Psalm 18:32–34a (NLT)

God isn't just interested in your success—He's ***invested*** in your success because you are an extension of Him. But His version of success is built on wisdom and strategy, not worrying and striving. Prayer is the portal where divine wisdom and strategy flow.

3. You Develop Boldness and Peace

Prayer shifts your posture. Even when circumstances are unstable, prayer reminds you that God is unshakable. You stop moving out of fear or desperation and begin to lead from a place of peace and authority. When you've spent time in the presence of God, you don't need external validation—you carry internal confidence.

"Don't worry about anything; instead, pray about everything. Tell God what you need, and thank him for all he has done. Then you will experience God's peace..."

— Philippians 4:6–7 (NLT)

"The wicked run away when no one is chasing them, but the godly are as bold as lions."

— Proverbs 28:1 (NLT)

Boldness doesn't mean arrogance. It means you're anchored. You don't panic when the numbers don't add up, because you're walking by faith, not fear. And that kind of leadership—anchored in peace—attracts favor and stability in your business.

4. You Create a Supernatural Culture

When prayer becomes part of your business rhythm, it permeates your brand, your workplace atmosphere, and your client experience. Your business becomes more than a service—it becomes a supernatural experience for everyone who comes in contact with it. Even unbelievers will recognize something different about how you operate. Your prayer life creates an environment where peace, integrity, and favor are felt— even if God's name is never spoken aloud.

"But the wisdom from above is first of all pure. It is also peace-loving, gentle at all times, and willing to yield to others... And those who are peacemakers will plant seeds of peace and reap a harvest of righteousness."

— James 3:17–18 (NLT)

"Let your good deeds shine out for all to see, so that everyone will praise your heavenly Father."

— Matthew 5:16 (NLT)

Prayer transforms your business from a transaction into a testimony. People won't just buy your product—they'll feel your peace, respect your values, and trust your leadership. Why? Because you've invited God to take the lead.

Practical Ways to Pray Over Your Business

- Pray before checking emails, making calls, or setting goals.
- Dedicate your first sale each month to God as a "first fruit."
- Cover your clients, your creativity, and your contracts in prayer.
- Create a "war room" space with your business name, mission, and scriptures posted.
- Keep a business prayer journal to track answered prayers and prophecies.

"Commit your actions to the Lord, and your plans will succeed."

— Proverbs 16:3 (NLT)

Let's be honest—there are days when you feel you're too overwhelmed to pray. The deadlines are mounting. The clients aren't paying. The launch flopped. The ideas dried up. In those moments, pray anyway.

"The earnest prayer of a righteous person has great power and produces wonderful results."

— James 5:16b (NLT)

Your prayer doesn't have to be long or eloquent. It just has to be honest. Invite God into your overwhelm. He's not intimidated by your frustration. He's not annoyed by your tears. You have a High Priest who is intimately aware of your pain and frustration He's the One who gave you the vision—and He'll sustain you through it.

Action Steps: Making Prayer a Business Priority

1. Block Prayer Time on Your Business Calendar

Set aside 15–30 minutes each workday to meet with God. Protect that time like you would a meeting with your biggest client. This is the most important step. DO NOT SKIP IT!!!

2. Write a Business Prayer Declaration

Create a personalized prayer you can speak daily over your business.

3. Identify 3 Business Areas You Need God to Move In

Be specific! Write them down and bring them to God in consistent prayer this week.

4. Track Your Prayers and Results

Start a "faith file" of answered prayers, unexpected favor, and divine strategies.

Prayer

Father God,

I thank You for trusting me with a business vision. I invite You into every corner of this assignment. Help me to pray before I plan and listen before I launch. I surrender my schedule, my ideas, and my income to You. Give me wisdom like Solomon, faith like Nehemiah, and clarity that can only come from Your Spirit. I declare that my business will be built on prayer, rooted in purpose, and fueled by grace. In Jesus' name, Amen.

Personal Notes or Prayers:

_____
_____
_____
_____
_____
_____
_____
_____
_____
_____
_____
_____
_____
_____
_____

Journal Pages
Chapter 2

Scripture to Meditate On
"Commit your actions to the Lord, and your plans will succeed."
— Proverbs 16:3 (NLT)

🧭Self-Check: My Current Prayer Habits
✔ Check all that apply:
☐ I pray before making business decisions
☐ I have a set time for business-focused prayer each day
☐ I journal or record answered prayers
☐ I often forget to involve God in business strategy
☐ I invite God into only the spiritual parts of life, not my business

In your own words, describe the current role prayer plays in your business:

_____

_____

_____

_____

_____

_____

_____

Journal Page
Chapter 2

Reflection Questions

1. When was the last time you prayed before a business decision? What was the result?

_____
_____
_____
_____

2. Which of the four outcomes of prayer (Clarity, Strategy, Boldness, Culture) do you most need right now? Why?

_____
_____
_____
_____

3. What divine strategies or ideas have you received in prayer that you haven't acted on yet?

_____
_____
_____
_____

Standalone Prayer Guide

Prayers for Kingdom Entrepreneurs —
Building by Faith, Not Flesh
Bonus Resource for Chapter 2

Morning Declaration Prayer

"The Lord directs the steps of the godly. He delights in every detail of their lives." **— Psalm 37:23 (NLT)**

Heavenly Father,
 Thank You for another day to walk in purpose. I surrender this day to You—my thoughts, my actions, and my business. Guide my conversations, my creativity, and my decisions. Let everything I do today reflect Your glory and excellence. I invite You into every corner of my company. Direct my steps and protect my peace. In Jesus' name, amen.

Prayer for Clarity and Direction

"Your word is a lamp to guide my feet and a light for my path."
— Psalm 119:105 (NLT)

Lord,
 I need Your wisdom today. There are ideas swirling in my mind, but I don't want to move without You. Speak clearly and guide me in the direction You've already prepared. Silence the noise of fear and competition. Align my heart with Your will, and make my next steps unmistakable. I trust You more than I trust the numbers. In Jesus' name, amen.

Prayer for Divine Strategy

"Call to me and I will answer you and tell you great and unsearchable things you do not know." **— Jeremiah 33:3 (NLT)**

God,

 You are the Master Strategist. Reveal Your blueprint for my business. Show me where to build, how to serve, and when to act. Give me strategies that don't make sense in the natural but lead to supernatural results. Download insight that no mentor or manual can provide. I trust that Your way is better than my best guess. Amen.

Prayer for Boldness and Peace

"Don't worry about anything; instead, pray about everything."
-Philippians 4:6 (NLT)

Father,

 There are moments when I doubt, when I worry, when I feel unqualified. Remind me that I'm not building alone. You are my Source and my Sustainer. Fill me with courage, confidence, and calm. Let peace guard my heart and boldness guide my decisions. I refuse to be intimidated by temporary setbacks. I will lead with faith. In Jesus' name, amen.

Prayer to Establish a Supernatural Culture

"Let your good deeds shine out for all to see, so that everyone will praise your heavenly Father." **— Matthew 5:16 (NLT)**

God,

 Let my business carry Your presence. Let every customer, partner, and employee experience something different—something holy. May my company be a refuge, a light, and a beacon of integrity. Let everything I touch be marked by prayer, excellence, and Your Spirit. May I never forget that I am a minister in the marketplace. Use me to glorify You. Amen.

CHAPTER 3

Living a Life of Integrity: Building a Business Based on Christian Values

"People with integrity walk safely, but those who follow crooked paths will be exposed." **— Proverbs 10:9 (NLT)**

Living a Life of Integrity: Building a Business Based on Christian Values

Integrity—The Foundation You Can't Fake

In a world driven by likes, leverage, and launch-day buzz, it's easy to think that the loudest brand wins. But in the Kingdom of God, the loudest voice is not the most powerful—the most rooted one is. And the root of any sustainable, God-honoring business? Integrity.

Integrity isn't just about avoiding lies or paying taxes on time. It's about being whole—undivided in your loyalty to God, consistent in your character, and unwavering in your commitment to doing what's right, even when it costs you.
Your gifts may get you in the room, but only integrity will keep you there. Your marketing may sell a product, but only integrity will build a legacy. Your favor may open doors, but without integrity, you'll eventually find yourself walking back out of them. Scripture says:

"People with integrity walk safely, but those who follow crooked paths will be exposed." **— Proverbs 10:9 (NLT)**

This isn't about perfection. It's about alignment—aligning your business practices with your faith, your pricing with your values, your partnerships with your purpose, and your service with God's standard, not just man's expectations.

Biblical Example
Joseph: From Pit to Palace with Integrity

Joseph's life is one of the most powerful case studies of integrity in the entire Bible. He didn't just survive injustice, he prospered through it; not by manipulation, wealth, or privilege, but by unwavering character and consistent obedience to God.

Integrity in Isolation

Before Joseph ever touched a throne, he was thrown into a pit by jealous brothers, sold into slavery, and falsely imprisoned. At every stage, Joseph had opportunities to compromise—to get ahead the world's way. But he didn't. When he was placed in Potiphar's house, he could have become bitter or dishonest. Instead:

"The Lord was with Joseph, so he succeeded in everything he did as he served in the home of his Egyptian master." — **Genesis 39:2 (NLT)**

Joseph treated someone else's house with the care and diligence he would give to his own. He honored Potiphar not because he had to, but because he honored God first. Even when Potiphar's wife tried to seduce him, Joseph didn't rationalize, negotiate, or give in to the secrecy of the moment. He didn't just fear consequences—he feared grieving God.

"How could I do such a wicked thing? It would be a great sin against God." — **Genesis 39:9 (NLT)**

This wasn't just about avoiding sin, it was about preserving purpose. Joseph understood that temporary pleasure could derail his eternal destiny.

Integrity in the Dark

What's more amazing is how Joseph maintained integrity even when things got worse, not better. After fleeing temptation, Joseph was imprisoned on false charges. Yet, even in prison:

"But the Lord was with Joseph in the prison and showed him His faithful love. And the Lord made Joseph a favorite with the prison warden." — **Genesis 39:21 (NLT)**

Joseph wasn't chasing influence, but his character kept attracting it. He didn't need a platform to be excellent. His integrity created one.

Integrity Unlocks Influence

Eventually, Joseph's consistent behavior caught the attention of Pharaoh. Not because he had a perfect résumé, but because he had a proven track record of discernment, humility, and reliability.
When Pharaoh had a disturbing dream no one could interpret, Joseph was summoned. He didn't boast. He didn't self-promote. He simply said: *"It is beyond my power to do this. But God can tell you what it means and set you at ease."* — **Genesis 41:16 (NLT)**

That moment changed everything. Joseph interpreted the dream, offered wisdom, and was immediately elevated from prisoner to prime minister.

"Then Pharaoh said to Joseph, 'Since God has revealed the meaning of the dreams to you, clearly no one else is as intelligent or wise as you are. You will be in charge of my court...'" — **Genesis 41:39–40 (NLT)**

His rise wasn't accidental; it was a direct result of integrity in the pit, excellence in obscurity, and humility in the spotlight.

Takeaway for Kingdom Entrepreneurs

Joseph didn't build a business. He built trust with God and with people. His story proves that:

- God sees your private integrity long before He rewards it publicly
- Your current environment doesn't have to be glamorous to be godly
- Integrity is the seed that grows favor in places you never expected

So, when clients ghost you, when competitors lie, when revenue dips, when no one sees the hours you're putting in—remain integrous. God is not looking for perfect entrepreneurs. He's looking for faithful stewards He can trust with influence, provision, and people.

What Integrity Looks Like in Business

Living a life of integrity in business isn't about perfection—it's about consistent obedience. It's making decisions rooted in honesty, fairness, humility, and accountability. It shows up in how you treat your clients, your contractors, your competitors—and yourself.
Let's break it down:

✓ Integrity is:

- Saying "no" to shortcuts that compromise your values
- Delivering what you promised—even if it's inconvenient
- Being transparent about mistakes and taking responsibility
- Refusing to manipulate or guilt people into buying
- Honoring contracts, boundaries, and timelines
- Not inflating your results or credentials to gain clout

"Let your yes be yes and your no be no." — **Matthew 5:37** (NLT paraphrased)

✗ Integrity is not:

- Ghosting clients or vendors
- Charging hidden fees or overpromising results
- Copying someone else's content and calling it your own
- Using spiritual language to guilt-trip people into purchasing

When integrity is your standard, your reputation becomes a magnet. Clients feel safe. Partners trust your word. And Heaven can trust you with more.

"If you are faithful in little things, you will be faithful in large ones..."
— Luke 16:10a (NLT)

Biblical Example:
Daniel's Integrity in a Corrupt System

Daniel served as a high-ranking government official under multiple kings in Babylon—a system known for idolatry and political corruption. Yet Daniel stood out because of his unshakable integrity. When jealous colleagues tried to destroy him, they couldn't find any dirt. Their only option was to create a law that would punish him for praying to God.

"They couldn't find anything to criticize or condemn. He was faithful, always responsible, and completely trustworthy." —
Daniel 6:4 (NLT)

Even under pressure, Daniel didn't fold. He kept praying. He didn't compromise. And what happened?

- God shut the mouths of lions.
- God promoted him after persecution.
- And God got the glory.

Daniel's story teaches us: You don't have to bend to win. You don't have to manipulate to succeed. If you remain faithful, God will fight for your reputation and your results.

When Integrity Costs You Something
Let's be honest—sometimes integrity comes at a price:
- You might lose a contract because you refused to lie.
- You might delay a launch because you refused to cut corners.
- You might get overlooked because you don't play dirty.

But that's where your faith kicks in.
"Better to have little, with godliness, than to be rich and dishonest." — **Proverbs 16:8 (NLT)**

You must decide early on: ***Do I want quick money or lasting impact?*** One builds a brand. The other builds a legacy. God is watching how you handle the small things. And when you pass the integrity test, He can elevate you without fear that you'll sabotage your own success.

Action Steps: Practicing Integrity Daily

1. **Conduct a Character Audit:** List any business practices that may need to be re-aligned with your values.

2. **Revisit Your Promises:** Are there unfulfilled promises to clients, team members, or partners that need to be addressed?

3. **Define Your Non-Negotiables:** Write out 3-5 values that guide every decision you make in your business.

4. **Create Accountability:** Who can you invite to lovingly hold you accountable to walk in integrity?

Prayer

Lord,

Help me to walk in integrity, even when it's not easy. I want my business to reflect Your righteousness, not just my ambition. Show me any area where I've compromised, and give me the courage to course-correct. Let me be trustworthy in small things so that You can entrust me with greater. Teach me to lead with honesty, humility, and boldness. I declare that I will build by faith—and with integrity. In Jesus' name, amen.

Personal Notes or Prayers:

_____
_____
_____
_____
_____
_____
_____
_____
_____
_____
_____
_____
_____

Integrity Values Worksheet
"Building a Business that Honors God"

Scripture to Meditate On
"If you are faithful in little things, you will be faithful in large ones..."
— Luke 16:10a (NLT)

Step 1: Define What Integrity Means to You
In your own words, describe what integrity means in your business context. Be detailed and specific.

_____

_____

_____

_____

_____

_____

_____

_____

Step 2: Evaluate Your Current Practices

For each of the following business areas, rate your alignment with integrity:

Business Area	Aligned with Integrity	Needs Improvement	Not Sure
Communication with Clients			
Pricing and Billing Practices			
Content Originality			
Follow Through on Commitments			
Marketing Language			
Business Contract			
Respecting Time and Boundaries			
Treatment of Team and Vendors			

Step 3: Identify Your Business Non-Negotiables

List 3–5 core values that you commit to never compromise—no matter the offer, client, or pressure.

1._____

_____

2._____

_____

3._____

_____

4._____

_____

5._____

_____

"A good reputation is more valuable than costly perfume."
— Ecclesiastes 7:1a (NLT)

Step 4: Realign Where Necessary

Is there any area where the Holy Spirit is convicting you to adjust your practices or make a wrong right?

☐ Yes

☐ No

If yes, what action will you take this week?

_____

_____

Who will you invite to lovingly hold you accountable?

_____

_____

Declaration of Integrity

Speak this aloud:

"I am a Kingdom entrepreneur. I am led by the Spirit, not by selfish gain. I commit to running my business with honesty, humility, and excellence. My word will be my bond. My reputation will reflect Christ.

I reject shortcuts, manipulation, and deceit. I choose integrity—even when no one is watching. I am building not just for now—but for legacy and for God's glory."

CHAPTER 4

Networking with a Purpose: Building Relationships in the Business World

"Walk with the wise and become wise; associate with fools and get in trouble." — **Proverbs 13:20 (NLT)**

Networking with a Purpose — Building Relationships in the Business World

In today's hyperconnected world, networking has become a buzzword tossed around in business circles as a measure of influence, reach, and success. But for the Kingdom entrepreneur, networking isn't just about collecting contacts or increasing visibility—it's about cultivating divine connections that serve God's plan for your life and business.

There is a distinct difference between networking to promote yourself and building relationships that align with purpose, obedience, and legacy. The world may chase collaborations for clout or cash, but in the Kingdom, partnerships are about assignment, alignment, and advancement—for both parties and for God's glory. When you network with purpose, you become a steward of relationships, not a manipulator of them.

CHAPTER 1

CHAPTER 2

CHAPTER 3

CHAPTER 4

"Walk with the wise and become wise; associate with fools and get in trouble." — **Proverbs 13:20 (NLT)**

Who you connect with can either launch you into your next level or delay your destiny. That's why discernment in your connections is not optional; it's essential. Kingdom collaboration isn't random—it's revelatory. You don't need a crowd; you need covenant relationships... people assigned to help you carry the vision, not dilute it.

In this chapter, we'll explore how to:
- Identify the difference between worldly networking and Kingdom collaboration
- Discern when a relationship is God-sent or self-serving
- Avoid the trap of transactional partnerships that lack spiritual integrity
- Build authentic, lasting connections rooted in mutual purpose and Kingdom principles

You are not called to build alone. God often delivers His promises through people, and those people are drawn to you not by force, but by faith and alignment. Let's uncover how to build with the right people, for the right reasons, at the right time.

The Power of Purposeful Relationships

In business, you will cross paths with many people—but not everyone is meant to walk alongside you. Purposeful relationships are those ordained by God, where alignment, values, timing, and assignment converge. These connections are not just about opportunity; they are about obedience. They pull you closer to your God-given destiny, not just toward a dollar sign.

"Two people are better off than one, for they can help each other succeed." **— Ecclesiastes 4:9 (NLT)**

Purposeful relationships:

- Refine you. They challenge your character and sharpen your discernment.
- Cover you. These people pray for you, not prey on you.
- Protect your vision. They don't compete with you—they complement you.
- Push you. They won't let you settle beneath your anointing.

How to Build Purposeful Relationships:

1. Pray before you partner. Never make permanent business connections without consulting God first. Ask: "Lord, is this connection an assignment or a distraction?"

2. Watch the fruit. Jesus said you'll know them by their fruit (Matthew 7:16). Are they consistent? Honest? Humble? Do they honor God in their own work?

3. Test alignment. Ask: "Do we share Kingdom values? Is this relationship mutually edifying?" If not, you may be forcing what was only meant to be a seasonal interaction.

4. Set boundaries early. Purposeful doesn't mean perfect. Clarify expectations, roles, and spiritual maturity to avoid unnecessary tension.

Ruth and Naomi: Covenant Connections That Birth Destiny

In the world of entrepreneurship, we're often taught to network for opportunity; to connect with people who can open doors, increase our reach, or give us access to platforms. But Ruth's story reminds us that God-ordained partnerships often look nothing like the world expects. Instead of seeking a powerful connection, Ruth committed to a purposeful relationship, one that required sacrifice, faith, and loyalty.

At first glance, Naomi had nothing to offer Ruth. She was a grieving, widowed mother-in-law, living in poverty and despair. No network. No income. No clear future. By all worldly standards, Ruth should have returned to Moab and started over. But she saw something deeper. She saw a purpose in their connection and a divine assignment that could only be fulfilled through obedient loyalty.

"But Ruth replied, 'Don't ask me to leave you and turn back. Wherever you go, I will go; wherever you live, I will live. Your people will be my people, and your God will be my God.'" **— Ruth 1:16 (NLT)**

This wasn't a transactional partnership, it was covenantal alignment.

1. Kingdom Collaboration vs. Worldly Networking
Worldly networking says, "What can you do for me?"
Kingdom collaboration says, "What can we build together for God's glory?"

Ruth didn't follow Naomi for status, success, or strategy—she followed her because she recognized that alignment with the right person in the right season could lead to divine breakthrough. She didn't need a full plan—just faith in the God Naomi served.

When you network God's way, the favor follows the relationship, not the résumé.

2. Discern God-Sent vs. Self-Serving Relationships
Many people come into your life because of what they perceive you can offer. But Ruth entered Naomi's life with no agenda. She didn't ask for anything in return—she simply offered loyalty. That kind of relationship is rare but essential for Kingdom entrepreneurs.

Ask yourself:
- Is this connection rooted in mutual purpose or personal gain?
- Do we share spiritual values, or is this a one-sided benefit?
- Is this partnership bearing fruit, or draining your focus?
-

Ruth wasn't after a blessing—she became a blessing, and because of that, God blessed her beyond what she could've imagined.

3. Avoiding Transactional Partnerships

Naomi had nothing to give Ruth materially. There were no hidden incentives or guarantees of provision. Ruth's devotion was not contingent on what she could gain, but on the God she had come to believe in through Naomi's life.

In business, it's easy to fall into relationships that are purely transactional:
- "If I promote you, you promote me."
- "If I share your post, will you endorse me?"
- "Let's collaborate—but only if your audience is bigger than mine."

These types of arrangements might feel beneficial in the short term, but they lack spiritual foundation and lasting fruit. Ruth teaches us to sow into relationships that carry Kingdom weight, not just earthly visibility.

4. Building Purposeful, Lasting Connections

Ruth's decision to stay with Naomi led to a chain of divine appointments:
- She gleaned in Boaz's field (by "coincidence" but really by God's hand)
- Boaz noticed her work ethic and character

- Naomi offered wisdom and guidance for navigating the opportunity
- Ruth and Boaz married and became part of the lineage of Jesus Christ

"So Boaz took Ruth into his home... The Lord enabled her to become pregnant, and she gave birth to a son... They named him Obed. He became the father of Jesse and the grandfather of David." — **Ruth 4:13, 17 (NLT)**

One covenantal relationship, grounded in faith and obedience, opened the door to legacy-level impact. Ruth wasn't just networking, she was walking in alignment.

Keys to Networking with Purpose

1. Pray First, Connect Second
Before you reach out to collaborate, promote, or pitch—pray.
 Ask God:
"Is this connection for covenant, commerce, or caution?"
"What role am I meant to play in their life?"
"Is this a seasonal connection or a long-term one?"

"The Lord directs the steps of the godly. He delights in every detail of their lives."— **Psalm 37:23 (NLT)**

2. Be the Connection You're Praying For
Don't just look for people to promote, fund, or support you. Be the answer to someone else's prayer. Serve. Refer. Encourage. Give freely, without always expecting something in return.

"Give, and you will receive. Your gift will return to you in full—pressed down, shaken together to make room for more..."
— Luke 6:38 (NLT)

Purposeful networking is a two-way street. When you become known as someone who adds value, honors time, and shows integrity, God will increase your influence and favor.

3. Discern Before You Collaborate
Not every opportunity is from God—even if it looks good. Some connections are distractions in disguise. Others may be misaligned in values, mission, or ethics.

Before you say yes to every event, partnership, or platform—pause and pray. Ask:

"Do our values align?"

"Is this an equally yoked connection?"

"Will this collaboration strengthen or dilute my message?"

"Don't team up with those who are unbelievers. How can righteousness be a partner with wickedness?" — **2 Corinthians 6:14a (NLT)**

This doesn't mean avoiding nonbelievers—but it does mean being wise about who has access to your influence.

What Purposeful Networking Produces

✔ Community instead of competition

✔ Collaboration that multiplies Kingdom impact

✔ Covenant relationships that sharpen your character

✔ Strategic introductions that open supernatural doors

"As iron sharpens iron, so a friend sharpens a friend."

— Proverbs 27:17 (NLT)

When you allow God to lead your relationships, you don't have to force your way into rooms. He will align you with the people who are already praying for what you carry—and who carry what you need.

Prayer

Father,

I thank You for divine relationships. Teach me how to build a network that honors You. Help me to connect with people who sharpen my faith, challenge my thinking, and multiply impact. Close every door that is not from You, and open every door that aligns with Your purpose for my life and business. Make me a trustworthy connection in someone else's story. I trust You to guide my conversations and assignments. In Jesus' name, amen.

Personal Notes or Prayers:

_____

_____

_____

_____

_____

_____

_____

_____

_____

_____

_____

_____

_____

Action Steps: Building Your Purposeful Network

Step 1: Identify 3 People You Feel Led to Connect With

1._____

2._____

3._____

Pray about your next step—reach out, encourage, serve, or ask for guidance.

Step 2. Review Your Current Network

Are there any connections God is calling you to release, redefine, or reinvest in?

3. Offer Value This Week

Look for one opportunity to help someone else in your network—without pitching or asking for anything in return.

Red Flags to Pray Over or Avoid When Making New Connections

Be cautious or seek further confirmation if you notice:
- A strong push to commit quickly without time for prayer
- A lack of transparency around finances, roles, or boundaries
- Manipulative language masked as "favor" or "divine connection"
- A reputation for inconsistency, gossip, or unethical practices
- Resistance to accountability, correction, or spiritual discernment

Bonus: Collaboration Commitments

If you move forward with the partnership, clarify the following with

your collaborator:

- Shared goals: _____

- Defined roles & responsibilities: _____

- Timeline & expectations: _____

- Honor code or boundaries: _____

- How will we resolve conflict biblically? _____

CHAPTER

Financial Stewardship:
Managing Your Business
Finances with Faith

"The earth is the Lord's, and everything in it. The world and all its people belong to him." **— Psalm 24:1 (NLT)**

Financial Stewardship: Managing Your Business Finances with Faith

Money is more than a medium of exchange—it is a mirror that reveals what we truly value. In the Kingdom of God, financial stewardship is not just about how much you earn; it's about how well you manage what you've been entrusted with. As Christian entrepreneurs, we are not owners—we are stewards. Everything we have comes from God and ultimately belongs to Him.

While the world often teaches us to chase profits at any cost, the Word teaches us to steward with purpose, obedience, and integrity. Business finances are spiritual before they are strategic. How you handle your income, expenses, giving, and growth reflects your heart posture toward God. Financial stewardship isn't just about bookkeeping—it's about kingdom keeping.

"To those who use well what they are given, even more will be given, and they will have an abundance." **— Matthew 25:29a (NLT)**

This chapter is not about restrictive budgeting or fear-based decisions. It's about learning to partner with God in your financial decisions so that your business not only flourishes but honors the One who blessed you with the opportunity in the first place.

CHAPTER 1

CHAPTER 2

CHAPTER 3

CHAPTER 4

CHAPTER 5

When we surrender our finances to God, we invite Him to lead us into supernatural provision and purposeful increase.

As you read this chapter, you'll be challenged to:
- Confront old money mindsets and embrace Kingdom principles
- Establish order in your business finances through structure and intentionality
- Tithe faithfully and give generously as acts of obedience and worship
- Create a plan that honors both your calling and your cash flow

You'll also discover the Key Pillars of Financial Stewardship in Business—a framework rooted in biblical wisdom that will help you handle money in a way that produces peace, profit, and purpose. You may have been taught to hustle harder, grind longer, and "make it happen" by any means necessary. But God's way is different. He invites us to prosper by faith, not fear. He wants to bless what we build—but first, He calls us to build it in alignment with His Word.

Let this chapter be the turning point where money stops being a source of stress and starts being a tool for obedience, impact, and legacy.

What Is Financial Stewardship?

Financial stewardship is more than paying bills and tracking income. It's the spiritual discipline of managing money according to God's principles and under the guidance of the Holy Spirit.

It involves:
- Honoring God with your increase
- Managing your expenses wisely
- Giving generously
- Saving and preparing for the future

- Avoiding debt traps and poor investments
- Operating your business with financial integrity

"Good planning and hard work lead to prosperity, but hasty shortcuts lead to poverty." — **Proverbs 21:5 (NLT)**

God Cares How You Handle Business Money

Many entrepreneurs believe that as long as they tithe personally, they've done their part. But if your business is part of your calling, then your business money is part of your ministry. And God is watching how you handle every dollar.

- Are you tithing from your business revenue or just your salary?
- Are you planning wisely or reacting emotionally?
- Are you pricing with prayer or people-pleasing?
- Are you paying people fairly or cutting corners?

The Bible is clear about tithing, we are instructed to tithe off of our increase. Increase includes every earned dollar, not just the ones earned from a salaried job. When you lean into tithing and stewarding your business increase well, you invite God to increase you and your business more and more.

"If you are dishonest in little things, you won't be honest with greater responsibilities." — **Luke 16:10 (NLT)**

You can't pray for financial overflow while ignoring financial stewardship. God blesses order, not chaos. If you do not do so already, pray for the wisdom to steward and invest your finances wisely. God has invited us all to live in financial overflow, from a place of abundance. It takes wisdom to navigate financial waters you've never been in before. It takes wisdom to learn which investments to take calculated risks on and which to avoid. The great thing for every Kingdom Entrepreneur is that God freely gives us all wisdom. It's our job to invite the spirit of wisdom into our finances.

Biblical Example: The Parable of the Talents (Matthew 25:14–30)

Jesus tells a story about a master who gave three servants different amounts of money to manage while he was away. Two of them invested and multiplied what they were given. One buried his out of fear. When the master returned, he rewarded the two who had stewarded wisely and called the one who hid his talent "wicked and lazy." Why? Because God expects multiplication, not just maintenance.

"You were faithful with a few things, so now I will put you in charge of many more things." **— Matthew 25:21 (NLT)**

This parable reminds us that fear is not an excuse for mismanaging God's resources. You have been called to increase If you want God to bless your business, show Him He can trust you to steward it with wisdom.

Key Pillars of Financial Stewardship in Business

1. Tithing and Giving: Honoring God First

"Honor the Lord with your wealth and with the best part of everything you produce." **— Proverbs 3:9 (NLT)**

Tithing is one of the clearest ways to show that God comes first—not just in words, but in finances. As a Kingdom entrepreneur, your business is not separate from your spiritual life. It's an extension of your calling. Therefore, what flows into your business should be tithed from the top, not from what's left over.

Practical Guidance:
- Decide where your tithe will go (your home church, ministry, or designated Kingdom projects).
- Set up automated tithing from your business checking account.
- Record your giving so you can testify to God's faithfulness later.
- Give offerings beyond the tithe as the Lord leads—especially when you sense He's calling you to stretch.

Reflection:
Am I treating my business income as sacred seed, or just survival money?
Do I trust God enough to give before I see how the month ends?

"Give freely and become more wealthy; be stingy and lose everything." — **Proverbs 11:24 (NLT)**

When you give, you break the spirit of fear over your finances and declare: God is my Source—not clients, not contracts, not cash flow.

2. Budgeting and Forecasting: Creating Structure for God to Bless

"Suppose one of you wants to build a tower. Won't you first sit down and estimate the cost to see if there is enough money to finish it?"
                                              — **Luke 14:28 (NLT)**

A budget is not a limit—it's a blueprint. You wouldn't build a house without architectural plans, so why build a business without financial ones? When you budget prayerfully, you create space for discipline, clarity, and ultimately peace. You know what's coming in, what's going out, and what needs to shift.

Practical Guidance:

- Set up a monthly income goal, then break it into weekly or daily sales targets.
- List out every recurring business expense, including tools, subscriptions, contractors, and software.
- Establish categories: tithes, savings, taxes, owner's pay, marketing, reinvestment.
- Use tools like Excel, Google Sheets, or financial apps (e.g., Wave, QuickBooks, YNAB).
- Revisit your numbers monthly, not just during tax season.

Reflection:

Am I stewarding my finances with the same excellence I expect from others? Have I asked God to bless what I haven't even tracked?

"Be sure you know the condition of your flocks; give careful attention to your herds..." **— Proverbs 27:23 (NLT)**

Budgeting isn't about control—it's about stewardship. It's how you count what God has given, so you can multiply what God will send next.

3. Saving and Investing Wisely: Planning for Legacy and Obedience

"The wise have wealth and luxury, but fools spend whatever they get." **— Proverbs 21:20 (NLT)**

As a Kingdom entrepreneur, your financial plan must go beyond just paying the bills or hitting sales goals. You need a long-term mindset. Saving isn't a lack of faith—it's the evidence of **wisdom.** And investing isn't only about money—it's about placing your resources where they can grow and expand the Kingdom. Lasting wealth isn't based on how well you earn. It's based on how well you save and invest.

Practical Guidance:
- Start by creating three savings accounts:
  - Emergency Fund (3–6 months of business expenses)
  - Purpose Fund (obedience money for when God says go)
  - Growth Fund (for new hires, rebranding, or development)
- Set up automatic transfers from your business account each month. (This can be as little as $5. Start where you are and grow from there)
- Reinvest a percentage of profit back into business education, systems, or equipment that increases efficiency.
- Don't wait until you're "making more" to start saving—start with discipline now.

Reflection:

Have I prepared my business to sustain a slow season, or am I living check to check in faith's name? Is God calling me to prepare for something that hasn't happened yet?

"Precious treasure and oil are in a wise man's dwelling, but a foolish man devours it." **— Proverbs 21:20 (NLT, paraphrased)**

You don't prepare after the door opens—you prepare so that you can walk through it when it does. Following the spirit of wisdom in your finances ensures you will always be prepared for what is to come.

4. Pricing with Prayer, Not Fear

"Those who work deserve their pay." **— Luke 10:7b (NLT)**

Pricing is spiritual. It reflects how you see your value, your assignment, and your trust in God to bring the right clients. Many Christian entrepreneurs underprice out of fear of rejection, guilt, or imposter syndrome—but low prices don't bless your business, and they don't bless your God. God is not glorified by burnout, over-delivery, or resentment. He is glorified by fairness, clarity, and confidence rooted in truth.

Practical Guidance:

- Pray over your pricing before finalizing your packages.
- Factor in time, transformation, deliverables, taxes, and tithing.
- Stop offering discounts from a place of fear or desperation.
- Know that charging fairly is not greed—it's stewardship.

"Do not cheat or rob anyone. Always pay your hired workers promptly." — **Leviticus 19:13 (NLT)**

Are you paying yourself like a worker in your own business?

Reflection:

Am I charging what the work is worth or what I think people will accept? Do I believe God can send people who will honor my value?

In Summary: The Fruit of Financial Stewardship

When you operate your business with biblical financial wisdom, you cultivate:

✔ Stability
✔ Peace
✔ Margin for generosity
✔ Room to grow
✔ Favor that follows order

"Then he entrusted the money to them while he was gone... The servant who received the five bags of silver began to invest the money and earned five more." — **Matthew 25:15–16 (NLT)**

You don't just want to be profitable—you want to be faithful. And that faithfulness starts with how you handle the resources God already gave you.

Prayer

Father,

You are the Giver of every good and perfect gift. Thank You for trusting me with this business. Teach me to be a wise steward. Help me to tithe in faith, plan with wisdom, and give generously. I reject fear, lack, and poverty mindsets. I choose order over chaos, strategy over stress, and obedience over greed. Let every dollar that flows through this business reflect Your glory and honor Your name. In Jesus' name, amen.

Personal Notes or Prayers:

_____

_____

_____

_____

_____

_____

_____

_____

_____

_____

_____

_____

_____

Financial Stewardship Roadmap:
Managing Your Business Finances with Faith

Pillar 1: Tithing & Giving

"Honor the Lord with your wealth and with the best part of everything you produce." **— Proverbs 3:9 (NLT)**

Core Truth:
Tithing is a spiritual principle that honors God as your source. Giving demonstrates trust, obedience, and generosity.

Action Steps:
- Tithe from business income consistently
- Automate your giving for discipline
- Create a giving plan (church, missions, causes)
- Track your giving as a testimony of faithfulness

Heart Check: Am I giving God my first, or my leftovers?

Pillar 2: Budgeting & Forecasting

"Be sure you know the condition of your flocks; give careful attention to your herds." **— Proverbs 27:23 (NLT)**

Core Truth:
Budgeting is not restrictive—it's revelatory. It allows you to see, plan, and prepare with clarity.

Action Steps:
- Build a monthly and quarterly budget
- Track income, tithes, expenses, and taxes
- Set sales goals and revenue targets
- Review your numbers monthly

Heart Check: Do I know where every dollar is going? Or am I "believing God" while mismanaging what He already gave?

Pillar 3: Saving & Investing Wisely

"The wise have wealth and luxury, but fools spend whatever they get." — **Proverbs 21:20 (NLT)**

Core Truth:
Saving shows wisdom. Investing shows faith for the future. Both prepare you to obey without delay.

Action Steps:
- Build three savings buckets:
- Emergency Fund · Obedience Fund · Growth Fund
- Reinvest in systems, education, and scalability
- Start small but stay consistent

Heart Check: Am I preparing for the door God hasn't opened yet?

Pillar 4: Pricing with Prayer, Not Fear

"Those who work deserve their pay." — **Luke 10:7 (NLT)**

Core Truth: Your price reflects your purpose and your trust in God. You're not selling—you're serving with excellence.

Action Steps:
- Pray over every price and package
- Price with integrity, not insecurity
- Stop discounting your calling out of fear
- Pay yourself as a laborer in your business

Heart Check: Am I apologizing for charging? Or do I believe I'm worth the value I deliver?

Faith + Order = Overflow

"Commit your actions to the Lord, and your plans will succeed."

— Proverbs 16:3 (NLT)

When you honor God with your finances, He can trust you with increase. Faithful stewardship leads to:

- Supernatural provision
- Peace over profit
- Confidence in decision-making
- Margin for generosity
- Legacy for generations

INCOME TRACKER

Month: _____

Project/Product	Client/Source	Income $
_____	_____	_____
_____	_____	_____
_____	_____	_____
_____	_____	_____
_____	_____	_____
_____	_____	_____
_____	_____	_____
_____	_____	_____
_____	_____	_____
_____	_____	_____
_____	_____	_____

Total Monthly Income

Income Source	Total $

Total Monthly $$$

TITHE TRACKER

Month: _____

DATE	TITHE AMOUNT	GIVEN TO:	NOTE/ SCRIPTURE

"Bring all the tithes into the storehouse..." — Malachi 3:10 (NLT)

MONTHLY FINANCIAL GOALS

What big goaI do I want to accomplish this month (Big Picture)?

TITHING GOALS

- [ ] _____
- [ ] _____
- [ ] _____

BUSINESS SAVINGS GOALS

- [ ] _____
- [ ] _____
- [ ] _____

PERSONAL SAVINGS GOALS

- [ ] _____
- [ ] _____
- [ ] _____

INVESTMENT GOALS

- [ ] _____
- [ ] _____
- [ ] _____

CHAPTER

Overcoming Adversity: Navigating Challenges and Setbacks in Your Business Journey

"When you go through deep waters, I will be with you. When you go through rivers of difficulty, you will not drown." **— Isaiah 43:2 (NLT)**

Overcoming Adversity: Navigating Challenges and Setbacks in Your Business Journey

Every Kingdom entrepreneur will, at some point, come face to face with adversity. It is not a matter of if, but when. The road to purpose-driven success is paved with obstacles, unexpected detours, and moments where giving up can seem more appealing than pressing on. But adversity is not the enemy—it is often the tool God uses to build the spiritual endurance, wisdom, and character needed to sustain your calling.

In business, adversity can take many forms: a failed launch, a major client walking away, financial strain, internal conflict, betrayal by trusted partners, or the deafening silence of delayed results. These challenges are not signs that you're off course—they may be confirmation that you're walking in purpose and the enemy is trying to wear you down.

"Dear brothers and sisters, when troubles of any kind come your way, consider it an opportunity for great joy." **— James 1:2 (NLT)**

God does not promise a life free from hardship, but He does promise to be with us in it. He does not remove every storm, but He gives us divine strategies to navigate through them without drowning. This chapter is not just a call to survive adversity—it is a call to grow through it, rise above it, and prosper in spite of it.

You'll be challenged to look at your struggles differently—not as setbacks, but as setups. You'll see how adversity sharpens your faith, cleanses your motives, and reveals your dependency on God. You'll be reminded that your trials are temporary, but the fruit they produce is eternal.

This chapter will also:
- Equip you with biblical examples of leaders who thrived through trials
- Help you identify the spiritual attacks masked as business roadblocks
- Offer you practical, prayerful steps to stay focused when things fall apart
- Remind you that adversity, when surrendered to God, is a catalyst for accelerated growth

Let this chapter stir your spirit and stabilize your resolve. You may bend—but you will not break. And when you come out on the other side, you won't just have success stories—you'll have testimonies.

The Inevitable Reality of Adversity

Adversity is not a detour in the life of the Kingdom entrepreneur—it's part of the curriculum. While the world sells an illusion of effortless success, God prepares us for a road that is narrow, sometimes rugged, but always redemptive. Whether it's financial difficulty, team betrayal, health challenges, unexpected losses, or spiritual warfare manifesting through business setbacks, adversity has a way of testing the authenticity of your calling. You'll be forced to answer the question: Did I start this business because God called me, or because I wanted more money? More money is a great secondary reason to start a business, but there are far easier ways to make more money. If your motivation isn't rooted in obedience to God, you will not be able to withstand the adversity that comes with owning a business.

"The godly may trip seven times, but they will get up again."
— Proverbs 24:16 (NLT

Resilience isn't just about being tough—it's about being anchored in God's Word when everything around you is shaking. This kind of faith doesn't deny hardship; it defeats it.

Now before we go further, let's dispel a common myth in the body of Christ. **Adversity is not always an attack—it can also be an assignment sent by God to assist you on your journey.** Like fire to gold, trials have a way of burning off what's impure and revealing what's been refined. It does not feel good, but it is necessary!

"So be truly glad. There is wonderful joy ahead, even though you must endure many trials for a little while." **— 1 Peter 1:6 (NLT)**

God does not waste adversity. He uses it to:
- Strengthen your prayer life (because sometimes pain is what gets us on our knees),
- Clarify your motives (adversity tests whether you're in this for God's glory or personal gain),
- Elevate your discernment (you learn who's really for you),
- And develop your capacity to lead.

Without adversity, you risk building a fragile success built on comfort. With it, you gain a foundation that can withstand growth. Remember the path of least resistance will always be attractive. However, building a business this way would be like building a skyscraper without steel. The building may go up quickly and easily, but the first major storm will cause it to come tumbling down.

Biblical Example:
Nehemiah — Adversity on Assignment

Nehemiah's story is one of purpose, pressure, and perseverance. He was not a priest, prophet, or warrior—he was a marketplace leader on divine assignment. His role as the king's cupbearer positioned him for influence, but his calling pulled him into a project far greater than his comfort zone: the rebuilding of Jerusalem's walls.

When Nehemiah heard that the walls of Jerusalem were broken down and its gates burned with fire, his heart broke—but his spirit burned with vision. He didn't run toward the problem recklessly; he began with prayer and planning (Nehemiah 1:4–11). This aligns with our teaching that adversity demands wisdom, spiritual sensitivity, and strategic stewardship.

Nehemiah did not face gentle opposition. From the moment he arrived in Jerusalem with permission to rebuild, he encountered mockery, threats, distractions, and plots to destroy him. His adversaries—Sanballat, Tobiah, and Geshem—used intimidation and slander to try and stop the work.

But Nehemiah didn't interpret the resistance as a sign that he was off course. He recognized it for what it was: confirmation that he was building something that mattered.

"They all made plans to come and fight against Jerusalem and throw us into confusion. But we prayed to our God and guarded the city day and night to protect ourselves." **— Nehemiah 4:8–9 (NLT)**

Adversity refined Nehemiah's resolve. He became more focused, more prayerful, and more dependent on God. Your adversity is not your enemy—it's an instrument God uses to forge your faith.

Trials Are Temporary, but the Fruit Is Eternal

The wall had been in ruins for decades, yet under Nehemiah's leadership, it was rebuilt in just 52 days (Nehemiah 6:15). That's not just strategy—that's supernatural acceleration. When you withstand the temporary trials, you open the door for God to award you with spoils of war. One of those spoils is speed. What may have taken others 10 years to build may only take you 10 months. When God's favor is upon your life, opposition doesn't stop the vision; it highlights God's favor.

"When our enemies and the surrounding nations heard about it, they were frightened and humiliated. They realized this work had been done with the help of our God." **— Nehemiah 6:16 (NLT)**

Nehemiah's perseverance produced eternal fruit—a restored city, a renewed people, and a testimony of God's power. Likewise, the adversity you're facing in business may be intense now, but it's producing fruit that will outlast the storm.

Adversity Will Purify Your Motives

Nehemiah's motives were constantly tested. Would he build for personal gain or for God's glory? Would he compromise when threatened? Would he abandon the mission for comfort? Each attack revealed what was in his heart—and purified it. When his enemies tried to distract him with a meeting, he refused, famously saying:

"I am engaged in a great work, so I can't come. Why should I stop working to come and meet with you?" **— Nehemiah 6:3 (NLT)**

When you're under pressure in business, your true motives rise to the surface. Will you still tithe when the revenue dips? Will you still honor your clients when your emotions are frayed? Nehemiah teaches us that adversity is a mirror, and a tool to refine your character and your "why."

Adversity Requires Both Spiritual Discernment and Practical Strategy

Nehemiah built with one hand and held a weapon in the other (Nehemiah 4:17). He combined faith and wisdom, prayer and planning, obedience and leadership.

"The laborers carried on their work with one hand supporting their load and one hand holding a weapon." **— Nehemiah 4:17b (NLT)**

You cannot overcome adversity with hustle alone. Nor can you win spiritual battles with strategy alone. Like Nehemiah, you must discern the moment and respond with both prayer and practical action.

This means building your business with excellence while remaining spiritually alert. It means creating systems while staying sensitive to divine redirection. Kingdom entrepreneurs do not choose between sword and strategy—we employ both.

Your Adversity is a Setup for Divine Endorsement

When the wall was finished, Nehemiah didn't ask for applause. But the entire region knew something miraculous had taken place. The result wasn't just a rebuilt wall—it was a public display of God's endorsement of His servant and His people. Your testimony—when you overcome adversity with integrity and faith—will speak louder than your pitch deck or marketing campaign. Like Nehemiah, what you build will become the evidence of what God has blessed.

Nehemiah didn't avoid adversity—he outlasted it through prayer, obedience, strategy, and holy boldness. His example reminds us that adversity doesn't cancel your assignment—it confirms it.

So take courage, Kingdom builder. Like Nehemiah, you are doing a great work that is setting you up for everlasting legacy. Remember it's not what we do in the natural that remains. What you do for God is what will last for generations to come. Don't think of your business as another thing you are doing to secure your family's future. You are responding to a divine need in the marketplace. You are being obedient to the instructions God has given you. That is your why. That is your motivator. The byproduct of your obedience is the success the business creates for you and your family. Always remember success is great byproduct of your obedience, but it is a horrible, grueling. relentless task master. If you don't believe me, ask some of the people who chased success over all else. Ask them how that worked out for them.

Nothing will purify your motives quite like adversity. It's the moment you will find out if you are doing this because you want money or fame, or if your motives are pure. When the adversity increases in business, many entrepreneurs return to the comforts of working for others, or begin to cut corners, but those of us who are committed to the assignment God has laid before us, do not run in the hard times. We double down in prayer, gain clarity, ask for wisdom, and move full steam ahead. Adversity will reveal whether you are "doing for the gram" or doing it for God!

Adversity will also deepen your dependency on God and reveal hidden idols. It's easy to say you depend on God when you know you have a paycheck hitting your account regularly, but can you also say the same when you have to depend on God for every new client, new book sale, or new product purchase? Can you still say you depend on God when the idol of traditional employment has taken up space in your heart? When something is stripped away, you learn what you've trusted too much. Adversity helps us to surrender every area of our lives to God so that we can let go of the things that no longer serve us and put things in their proper place in our hearts.

Adversity also helps us recognize our spiritual authority. **NOTHING** will push you to your knees in prayer or force you to exercise the gift of spiritual authority like entrepreneurship. Adversity in entrepreneurship will teach you how to take control of the atmosphere, your business, and the Earth realm!

Prayer

Heavenly Father,

I come to You today not from a place of defeat, but from a place of faith. Though adversity surrounds me, I choose to trust in Your unfailing Word. You are not surprised by my struggles, and You have not forgotten the vision You placed inside of me.

You are the God who sees, the God who restores, and the God who promotes. I ask You now to help me endure the hardships I face in my business with grace, clarity, and spiritual discernment. Let every obstacle become an opportunity to rely more deeply on You. Your Word says, *"When troubles of any kind come your way, consider it an opportunity for great joy."* **– James 1:2 NLT**

Help me find joy in this process—not because it's easy, but because it is evidence that You are shaping something greater in me. Refine my motives. Increase my wisdom. Purge pride, fear, and frustration. Replace them with peace, strategy, and supernatural strength.

Father, like Nehemiah, help me to keep building even when I am under pressure. Teach me to war in the spirit and work with excellence. Give me divine endurance so that I don't just survive this season—I thrive through it.

Send me kingdom-aligned help. Silence every voice of doubt. And most of all, Lord, be glorified in how I respond to difficulty. Let my testimony shine brighter than the trial. I declare that this adversity is not the end—it is a setup for increase, influence, and impact.

In Jesus' Name,
Amen.

Reflection Worksheet: Pressing Through Adversity

Take 15–30 minutes in prayerful reflection to complete the following prompts. This is a time for honest evaluation, emotional processing, and strategic insight.

1. What adversity am I currently facing in my business?

(List the main challenges you're experiencing right now. Be specific.)

_____

_____

_____

_____

_____

_____

2. How have I responded to these challenges so far—mentally, emotionally, and spiritually?

(Have you drawn closer to God or pulled away? Have you stayed consistent or wavered?)

_____

_____

_____

_____

_____

_____

3. What scripture from this chapter encourages me the most? Why?

(Write the full verse and explain what it speaks to in your current season.)

_____

_____

_____

_____

_____

4. What lesson is God trying to teach me through this adversity?

(Be still. Ask the Holy Spirit to show you what needs to grow or shift.)

_____

_____

_____

_____

_____

5. What strategy can I apply this week to push through adversity?

☐ Return to the original vision
☐ Create or update my prayer strategy
☐ Delegate or restructure operations
☐ Take a day of rest and spiritual renewal
☐ Meet with a trusted advisor
☐ Other: _____

6. Declare Your Faith:

Finish this sentence in your own words:

"Even though I'm going through _____, I believe God is going to _____."

CHAPTER 7

Making a Difference: Using Your Business to Make a Positive Impact in Your Community and the World

"Let your good deeds shine out for all to see, so that everyone will praise your heavenly Father." — **Matthew 5:16 (NLT)**

Making a Difference: Using Your Business to Make a Positive Impact in Your Community and the World

Introduction: Profit is Good, but Purpose is Greater

You didn't build this business just to make money—you built it to make impact. Every vision begins with a spark—a whisper from Heaven that says, "There's more in you." For some, it began as an idea scribbled in a notebook. For others, it was born out of frustration with systems that failed people, or a burden to see change where others only saw problems. However it started, your business is not a random pursuit—it's a divine assignment.

As a Kingdom entrepreneur, your business is more than a brand. It's a beacon. A ministry. A marketplace assignment. You have been entrusted with influence, not for self-promotion, but for Kingdom expansion. God placed you in the marketplace so His light could shine through your creativity, your service, and your success. Every product you design, every service you offer, and every client interaction is a potential altar—a moment for God's glory to meet human need.

There is nothing wrong with profit. Profit is necessary. It sustains operations, supports your family, and allows you to employ others. But profit alone cannot fulfill the deepest calling inside of you. You were wired for purpose.

Profit feeds your business. Purpose fuels your soul.

When you understand that distinction, your goals shift. You stop asking, "How much can I make?" and start asking, "How much difference can I make?" You begin to see revenue as a resource and influence as an instrument. Your success becomes a seed—something that multiplies beyond yourself. Because here's the truth: God didn't just call you to succeed—He called you to serve.

"God has given each of you a gift from his great variety of spiritual gifts. Use them well to serve one another." **—1 Peter 4:10 (NLT)**

Your business is one of those gifts. It's a unique expression of how God designed you to reflect His love, His wisdom, and His excellence in a world that desperately needs all three. When you work with purpose, you turn ordinary transactions into eternal impact. Clients become divine connections. Opportunities become open doors for ministry.

Purpose keeps you grounded when profit fluctuates. It reminds you that even on the slow days, you're still in alignment with Heaven's plan. It gives meaning to the grind and peace in the process, because you know that what you're building has eternal value. When you begin to see your business as a platform to bless others, you'll find that impact becomes the new income.

God starts to measure your success not just by how high your numbers climb, but by how deeply your obedience flows. Your value won't be defined by how many clients you serve—but by how faithfully you serve each one.

In a world obsessed with gain, you've been called to give.
In a culture chasing fame, you've been chosen to reflect faith.
And in a marketplace consumed with competition, you've been anointed for compassion.

You are not just a business owner—you are a Kingdom builder. And when you operate from that truth, profit will follow purpose every single time.

The Kingdom Standard for Business Impact

There's a difference between being successful and being significant. Success is measured in numbers—sales, followers, reach, and revenue. Significance is measured in impact—the lives changed, the hope restored, and the faith awakened because you obeyed God's call to create. Many people chase after success, but few pursue significance. The world celebrates achievement, but Heaven celebrates alignment. When you build according to God's blueprint, your work stops being about what you can get and starts being about who you can become through your service to others.

Success fills your account. Significance fills the earth with the presence of God.
Success brings comfort. Significance brings transformation.
Success makes your name known. Significance makes His name known.

As a Kingdom entrepreneur, you are not called to blend in—you are called to raise the standard. You represent a different kind of excellence, one that is rooted in integrity and driven by purpose. Your business is not just competing in a market; it's advancing the Kingdom.

The impact-driven business owner doesn't just ask how to grow their brand—they ask:
- Who can I serve through this product or service?
- How can I lift up others as I climb?
- What injustice or need can my work help solve?
- How can I use my platform to bring light where there is darkness?

These questions shift your business from transactional to transformational. You stop seeing clients as customers and start seeing them as assignments. You stop chasing visibility and start pursuing value.

You stop striving for success in the world's eyes and begin aligning with Heaven's agenda. That's the Kingdom standard... to build something on earth that reflects the heart of Heaven. When your business culture mirrors God's character, excellence becomes evangelism. When people experience integrity, compassion, and love through your work, they get a glimpse of the Father's heart. You are, in essence, doing ministry—one decision, one conversation, and one act of service at a time.

"Whatever you do or say, do it as a representative of the Lord Jesus..."
— Colossians 3:17 (NLT)

This means every business decision... how you price, how you communicate, how you deliver, becomes a reflection of who you represent. You don't need a pulpit to preach when your work ethic and grace-filled approach speak volumes. You are Heaven's ambassador in the marketplace. Your words carry weight. Your work carries witness. And your business, when done God's way, carries the aroma of Christ wherever it goes.

The Kingdom standard doesn't just change how you build—it changes why you build. You begin to see that your vision is part of a much larger story. The profits you generate, the influence you gain, and the people you serve are all threads in a divine tapestry God is weaving through your obedience. When you lead from that revelation, you understand that you're not just managing a company—you're managing a calling. And when the calling drives the company, impact becomes inevitable.

The Proverbs 31 Woman

When people talk about the Proverbs 31 woman, they often focus on her diligence, her skill, and her ability to "get it all done." But if you look deeper, her true strength was not found in her busyness—it was found in her balance.

She worked hard, yes, but her heart remained anchored in purpose. Her hands created wealth, but her spirit extended compassion. She was not simply a homemaker—she was a history maker.

She was not just industrious, she was impactful.

The Bible says that she "carefully watches everything in her household and suffers nothing from laziness" (Proverbs 31:27, NLT). She was a steward of both her time and her talent. She understood that the gifts God gave her were not for vanity but for victory; victory over lack, over fear, and over limitations that often hold women back. She rose early, worked with willing hands, and used her creativity to provide for her family. But what made her remarkable wasn't simply her ability to produce, it was her willingness to pour out. She didn't hoard her prosperity; she shared it. She didn't just manage her business; she ministered through it.

"She extends a helping hand to the poor and opens her arms to the needy." **— Proverbs 31:20 (NLT)**

That verse captures the heart of a Kingdom entrepreneur. Her business wasn't just profitable, it was purposeful. She understood that abundance is not complete until it blesses someone else. Her wealth had wings because her heart had wisdom.

Notice the order of her impact:
1. She managed her household with excellence. Her first ministry was home.
2. She invested and ran profitable ventures. She bought fields, planted vineyards, and worked with merchants.
3. She extended her hand to the poor. Her overflow became outreach.

She was both wise and generous, an investor and an intercessor, a provider and a philanthropist. Her example shows that spiritual devotion and entrepreneurial success are not opposites, they are allies.

Her faith informed her business, and her business reflected her faith.

The Proverbs 31 woman teaches us that Godly success is holistic. It touches your home, your work, and your community. She wasn't known just for what she owned—she was known for what she gave.
And isn't that the essence of Kingdom impact? Prosperity that doesn't stop with you but flows through you. Influence that doesn't inflate ego but amplifies generosity. Work that doesn't just build a name but builds the Kingdom. Her story invites us to reimagine what success looks like.

True prosperity is not measured by how much we accumulate, but by how many lives are better because we obeyed God's call to serve. Like the Proverbs 31 woman, we are called to build businesses that are both fruitful and faithful. Enterprises that reflect Heaven's order: strong, generous, wise, and full of grace.

She was the original example of what happens when faith meets strategy and purpose meets profit. She showed us that you can be spiritual and successful, prayerful and prosperous, anointed and accomplished, all at the same time. Her life reminds us that when God blesses the work of your hands, the true measure of that blessing is how far your hands reach.

Ways Your Business Can Make a Difference
The beauty of Kingdom entrepreneurship is that impact isn't reserved for those with massive platforms or million-dollar revenues. Every act of obedience, every service rendered with integrity, every client treated with honor is a seed that Heaven recognizes.

You don't have to wait until you've "arrived" to make a difference.
You make a difference as you build.
You impact lives as you grow.
You advance the Kingdom as you obey.

Below are five ways to infuse your business with purpose and ensure your success carries eternal significance.

1. Serve Your Clients with Excellence and Integrity

Impact begins at the point of service. Before your message reaches the masses, it must first reach the people in front of you. How you treat your clients—especially when no one is watching—speaks volumes about who you truly serve. Excellence is not about perfection. It's about intentionality. It's showing up on time, following through on promises, and treating each client interaction as an opportunity to reflect the nature of Christ.

When you operate with integrity, you stand out in a world where shortcuts are celebrated and self-interest often overshadows service. Your clients can feel the difference when your motivation is rooted in love instead of ambition. They may not always understand your faith, but they'll always recognize your fruit.

Ask yourself:
- Do my clients feel valued and heard after working with me?
- Do my business systems reflect order, honesty, and fairness?
- Would God be pleased with the way I represent Him through my brand?

You don't need a church building to do ministry.

Every consultation, every project, every sale is a chance to serve with the heart of Christ.

"Do to others whatever you would like them to do to you."

— Matthew 7:12 (NLT)

When your clients feel cared for, you create more than a transaction—you create transformation. Your reputation becomes a witness. Your service becomes a sermon. And your excellence becomes an offering to God.

2. Give Back Through Generosity

Generosity is one of Heaven's greatest investments. Every time you give, you declare that God—not money—is your source. You may not be able to fund every cause, but you can be faithful with what you have. Whether it's donating a percentage of your profits, offering scholarships, providing discounted services to ministries, or sponsoring community events, every act of giving echoes eternity.

Your generosity doesn't go unnoticed by Heaven. It plants spiritual seeds that multiply in ways you can't always measure. What you release leaves your hand, but it never leaves your life. God finds ways to return it—pressed down, shaken together, and running over.

"You must each decide in your heart how much to give... For God loves a person who gives cheerfully." — **2 Corinthians 9:7 (NLT)**

When you sow cheerfully, your giving becomes an act of worship. It says, "Lord, I trust You more than my balance sheet." And here's the Kingdom secret: generosity doesn't just bless others—it strengthens your faith. It realigns your focus from self-sufficiency to God-dependency. It reminds you that you're not the owner—you're the steward. Whether you give time, money, or resources, your business becomes a vessel through which God's goodness flows into the earth.

3. Mentor the Next Generation

Every Kingdom builder is also a Kingdom bridge. Someone poured into you—now it's your turn to pour into someone else. Mentorship is one of the most powerful forms of impact because it multiplies wisdom.

When you teach others what God has taught you, you accelerate their growth and redeem your own experiences. Even your mistakes become ministry when they help someone else avoid the same pitfalls.

Ask yourself:
- Who can benefit from the lessons I've learned?
- Who is watching me, even if I don't realize it?
- Who can I empower through conversation, encouragement, or opportunity?

Mentorship doesn't always look formal. It can happen over coffee, during a Zoom call, or in the form of content that uplifts and teaches. Sometimes the greatest mentorship moments come when you simply share your story honestly. Mentorship is impact in seed form. The people you pour into today become the leaders who shape tomorrow. The wisdom you release now will bear fruit long after your business season changes.

Every generation of Kingdom entrepreneurs should leave the next one stronger, wiser, and more equipped to carry God's vision forward.

4. Champion Righteousness in the Marketplace
In today's business world, compromise often comes disguised as "strategy." But the Kingdom entrepreneur understands that no success is worth the cost of integrity. You are not called to blend into the culture—you are called to be the culture changer. That means standing firm in your convictions even when it's unpopular. It means treating employees fairly, paying people on time, telling the truth even when it costs you, and making decisions that honor God rather than manipulate outcomes.

Integrity is the loudest sermon you will ever preach in the marketplace. People may not agree with your faith, but they will respect your consistency.

"Those who lead many to righteousness will shine like the stars forever." **— Daniel 12:3 (NLT)**

Your business can be a light in dark industries, a place where ethics are restored and fairness is practiced. When you stand for righteousness, you give others permission to do the same. You shift atmospheres. You influence culture. You remind the world that holiness and success can coexist.

Let your light shine—not by shouting your beliefs—but by living them out daily. Quiet integrity is louder than prideful promotion.

5. Partner With Kingdom Causes

Partnership multiplies power. When you align your business with God's causes—missions, community outreach, church initiatives, or humanitarian projects—you extend your reach far beyond your own audience. Imagine your business profits funding clean water wells, school supplies for underprivileged children, or disaster relief efforts. Picture your services empowering ministries, supporting single mothers, or sending missionaries overseas. Every collaboration becomes a Kingdom connection that turns commerce into compassion.

When you partner with God's purposes, you don't just gain favor—you activate spiritual backing. Heaven endorses what Heaven inspires. Partnership is also a reminder that we are part of a much bigger picture. It dismantles isolation and builds community among believers who are advancing God's Kingdom through their diverse gifts. When you link arms with others who share your values, you strengthen the entire body of Christ.

Together, your light shines brighter, your reach grows wider, and your business carries eternal weight.

When you lead your business with a heart for impact, God ensures your influence outlasts your income. The world doesn't just need more entrepreneurs—it needs Kingdom entrepreneurs. Men and women who understand that their prosperity is a vehicle for God's purposes. Every product, every policy, every plan can become a pathway to change. And when you choose to build with Heaven's blueprint, your business won't just succeed—it will shine.

Closing Reflection: The Ripple Effect of Obedience

Every act of obedience sends a ripple into eternity. You may not see where those ripples travel, but Heaven records every one. When you choose to run your business God's way—when you honor Him with your decisions, your ethics, your giving, and your grace—you release a chain reaction that outlives you. People you'll never meet will be blessed because you said "yes" to what He called you to build.

Sometimes the impact you make will be visible: the client who finds confidence through your coaching, the family fed through your generosity, the employee whose life changes because you believed in their potential. Other times, your obedience will work quietly beneath the surface—transforming hearts, shifting cultures, and restoring hope where despair once lived.

But whether seen or unseen, your obedience always bears fruit. It's easy to underestimate what God can do through one faithful entrepreneur. But Scripture reminds us that a single seed, when planted in good soil, produces a harvest thirty, sixty, even a hundred times more than what was sown. Your consistency is the seed. Your integrity is the water. Your faith is the sunlight. And God is the One who brings the increase.

There will be seasons when obedience costs more than it seems to give. You may have to turn down opportunities that compromise your values. You may have to forgive clients who wronged you or sow resources when you feel stretched thin. Yet even in those moments, you can rest in the promise that obedience never ends in loss—it ends in legacy.

God is not just building a business through you; He's building a testimony. One that says, "This is what happens when purpose leads profit and faith guides function. Your business becomes a living altar, a place where Heaven and earth meet through your daily decisions. Every invoice paid with integrity, every product created with excellence, every partnership formed in prayer becomes an act of worship. You are proving that faith and commerce can coexist, that success and surrender are not enemies, and that God's way is still the best way.

**You were not called just to build wealth,
you were called to build witness.**

**You were not called just to make noise,
you were called to make impact.**

**And you were not called just to achieve,
you were called to advance the Kingdom.**

The ripple of your obedience will touch people you'll never know, in places you'll never go. And when your time on earth is done, Heaven will show you the faces of those whose lives were changed because you chose to build with both hands open—one to receive from God and the other to release what He gave you.

So, keep serving. Keep sowing. Keep shining. Because when Kingdom entrepreneurs walk in purpose, profit follows and glory leads.

"The Weight of My Witness"

Take a quiet moment with God and reflect on this question:

"If my business disappeared tomorrow, what evidence would remain that I served, loved, and led with the heart of Christ?"

Write honestly about what that would look like.
Would people remember your products or your presence? Your excellence or your empathy? Your success or your surrender to God's will?

Ask the Holy Spirit to show you:
- Where your business currently makes impact—and where He's inviting you to go deeper.
- How your daily decisions reflect His character to those you serve.
- What legacy of light He wants your work to leave in the earth.

_____

_____

_____

_____

_____

_____

_____

_____

_____

"The Weight of My Witness"

Finish this sentence in the space below:

"My business will glorify God by..."

Let your answer flow freely, without editing. This may become the mission statement Heaven writes on your heart.

_____

_____

_____

_____

_____

_____

_____

_____

_____

_____

_____

_____

A Prayer for Prosperous Purpose

Heavenly Father,

Thank You for every seed of wisdom You've planted within these pages and within the heart of every reader. Thank You for reminding us that true prosperity is not measured by possessions, but by purpose; not by status, but by service; not by gain, but by giving. Lord, we offer back to You the vision, the business, and the dreams You have entrusted to our care. We surrender our plans so that Your divine strategy can take the lead. Let every idea be inspired by Heaven, every product be touched by compassion, and every service be marked by excellence that reflects Your glory.

Father, make us Kingdom entrepreneurs who build with clean hands and pure hearts. Teach us to pursue profit with integrity and to prioritize purpose with joy. Help us to see people before profit, ministry before marketing, and impact before income. May our obedience echo beyond our lifetime and our work become a light that draws others to You.

When challenges arise, remind us that wisdom is our anchor and faith is our foundation. When doors close, remind us that You are the God of divine redirection. When success comes, remind us to stay humble, grateful, and generous—always pointing back to You as the source of every blessing.

Lord, we dedicate our businesses, our talents, and our influence to Your Kingdom. Let every contract, every conversation, and every connection advance Your will in the earth. And when the world sees what we build, may they see not just our skill, but Your Spirit at work through us. May our lives declare: "God did this." May our success testify that faith still works. And may our legacy be one of wisdom, service, and impact that glorifies Your name. In Jesus' mighty name we pray, Amen.

Declaration of Faith

"Lord, I believe that You are the source of my vision, the author of my strategy, and the sustainer of my success. I dedicate my business, my gifts, and my goals to You. I will walk in wisdom, operate in integrity, and lead with love. I will use my influence to lift others, and my prosperity to glorify You. I am not chasing success; I am cultivating significance. I am not working for money, I am working for the mission You have trusted me to complete. Everything I have belongs to You, and everything I do will point back to You. This is my season to prosper by faith, and I will walk it out with purpose, passion, and peace."

I decree and declare by the authority given to me in the book of Genesis, that everything I need to complete the task set before me is in my hands, in my mouth, and in my ability to hear clearly from Heaven. My business prospers because I see the wisdom of God in every area and apply that wisdom to make every decision. I call forth every client, staff member, sponsor, vendor, team member, and associate needed to grow this business to the level of success God desires for me to experience. God guides my expansion through His word as I purposely partner with the spirit of wisdom. In the mighty name of Jesus, I decree and declare that I will see what I have said, in Jesus' name, Amen!

Final Reflection:
My Prosperity by Faith Declaration

Before you close this book, take a deep breath and allow yourself to rest in the presence of God.

Everything you've read, written, and reflected upon has been preparing you for this moment... the moment where revelation becomes response.

This is where faith becomes action.
This is where wisdom becomes a way of life.
This is where your business becomes your ministry.

Take a few moments to write your personal declaration of faith and purpose. Let it be honest, bold, and filled with expectancy. Write it as a covenant between you and God; a commitment to build, lead, and prosper according to His will.

_____

_____

_____

_____

_____

_____

_____

_____

_____

_____

_____

About the Author

Otescia R. Johnson is a bestselling author, publisher, speaker, business mentor, and transformational coach with a passion for helping believers prosper by faith, walk in wisdom, and fulfill their divine purpose in the marketplace.

As the founder of B.O.Y. Enterprises, Otescia has spent nearly a decade empowering Kingdom-minded authors and entrepreneurs to turn their God-given ideas into thriving, profitable businesses. With more than nineteen published books and journals, she has established herself as a leading voice in Christian entrepreneurship—bridging biblical principles with practical business strategy.

Otescia is also the visionary behind several life-changing programs and events, including the CEO Arise Conference, which gathers Kingdom entrepreneurs for empowerment and strategic growth, and the Broke to Profitable Group Coaching Program, which helps individuals move from financial frustration to sustainable success through faith-based systems and stewardship. She is also the creator of the Wisdom Seekers Program, a transformational experience that equips believers to hear God's voice in business and apply His wisdom to every area of life.

Known for her transparent teaching style and powerful storytelling, Otescia combines biblical truth, business insight, and personal testimony to inspire others to lead with excellence and build with eternal impact. Her message is simple but powerful: you are not just called to make money—you are called to make a difference. Whether through books, workshops, or one-on-one coaching, Otescia continues to mentor leaders, authors, and visionaries who are ready to grow spiritually, lead strategically, and prosper by faith.

To book Otescia R. Johnson for speaking engagements, classes, workshops, or private coaching, please visit www.otesciajohnson.com or email Otescia directly at orjohnson@alwaysbetonyourself.com

Bonus!

What has God said to me about this business?

GOD'S
DECREE

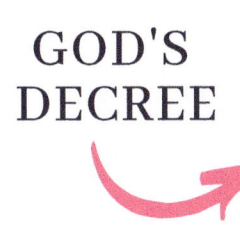

_____

_____

_____

_____

_____

_____

_____

_____

_____

_____

_____

_____

_____

_____

_____

_____

_____

_____

_____

_____

_____

_____

_____

MONTHLY FINANCIAL GOALS

What big goaI do I want to accomplish this month (Big Picture)?

TITHING GOALS

- ☐ _____
- ☐ _____
- ☐ _____

BUSINESS SAVINGS GOALS

- ☐ _____
- ☐ _____
- ☐ _____

PERSONAL SAVINGS GOALS

- ☐ _____
- ☐ _____
- ☐ _____

INVESTMENT GOALS

- ☐ _____
- ☐ _____
- ☐ _____

TITHE TRACKER

Month: _____

DATE	TITHE AMOUNT	GIVEN TO:	NOTE/ SCRIPTURE

"Bring all the tithes into the storehouse..." — Malachi 3:10 (NLT)

MONTHLY FINANCIAL GOALS

What big goaI do I want to accomplish this month (Big Picture)?

TITHING GOALS

- [ ] _____
- [ ] _____
- [ ] _____

BUSINESS SAVINGS GOALS

- [ ] _____
- [ ] _____
- [ ] _____

PERSONAL SAVINGS GOALS

- [ ] _____
- [ ] _____
- [ ] _____

INVESTMENT GOALS

- [ ] _____
- [ ] _____
- [ ] _____

TITHE TRACKER

Month: _____

DATE	TITHE AMOUNT	GIVEN TO:	NOTE/ SCRIPTURE

"Bring all the tithes into the storehouse..." — Malachi 3:10 (NLT)

MONTHLY FINANCIAL GOALS

What big goaI do I want to accomplish this month (Big Picture)?

TITHING GOALS

- [ ] _____
- [ ] _____
- [ ] _____

BUSINESS SAVINGS GOALS

- [ ] _____
- [ ] _____
- [ ] _____

PERSONAL SAVINGS GOALS

- [ ] _____
- [ ] _____
- [ ] _____

INVESTMENT GOALS

- [ ] _____
- [ ] _____
- [ ] _____

TITHE TRACKER

Month: _____

DATE	TITHE AMOUNT	GIVEN TO:	NOTE/ SCRIPTURE

"Bring all the tithes into the storehouse..." — Malachi 3:10 (NLT)

MONTHLY FINANCIAL GOALS

What big goaI do I want to accomplish this month (Big Picture)?

TITHING GOALS

- [ ] _____
- [ ] _____
- [ ] _____

BUSINESS SAVINGS GOALS

- [ ] _____
- [ ] _____
- [ ] _____

PERSONAL SAVINGS GOALS

- [ ] _____
- [ ] _____
- [ ] _____

INVESTMENT GOALS

- [ ] _____
- [ ] _____
- [ ] _____

TITHE TRACKER

Month: _____

DATE	TITHE AMOUNT	GIVEN TO:	NOTE/ SCRIPTURE

"Bring all the tithes into the storehouse..." — Malachi 3:10 (NLT)

MONTHLY FINANCIAL GOALS

What big goaI do I want to accomplish this month (Big Picture)?

TITHING GOALS

- [ ] _____
- [ ] _____
- [ ] _____

BUSINESS SAVINGS GOALS

- [ ] _____
- [ ] _____
- [ ] _____

PERSONAL SAVINGS GOALS

- [ ] _____
- [ ] _____
- [ ] _____

INVESTMENT GOALS

- [ ] _____
- [ ] _____
- [ ] _____

TITHE TRACKER

Month: _____

DATE	TITHE AMOUNT	GIVEN TO:	NOTE/ SCRIPTURE

"Bring all the tithes into the storehouse..." — Malachi 3:10 (NLT)

MONTHLY FINANCIAL GOALS

What big goaI do I want to accomplish this month (Big Picture)?

TITHING GOALS

- [ ] _____
- [ ] _____
- [ ] _____

BUSINESS SAVINGS GOALS

- [ ] _____
- [ ] _____
- [ ] _____

PERSONAL SAVINGS GOALS

- [ ] _____
- [ ] _____
- [ ] _____

INVESTMENT GOALS

- [ ] _____
- [ ] _____
- [ ] _____

TITHE TRACKER

Month: _____

DATE	TITHE AMOUNT	GIVEN TO:	NOTE/ SCRIPTURE

"Bring all the tithes into the storehouse..." — Malachi 3:10 (NLT)

MONTHLY FINANCIAL GOALS

What big goaI do I want to accomplish this month (Big Picture)?

TITHING GOALS

- [ ] _____
- [ ] _____
- [ ] _____

BUSINESS SAVINGS GOALS

- [ ] _____
- [ ] _____
- [ ] _____

PERSONAL SAVINGS GOALS

- [ ] _____
- [ ] _____
- [ ] _____

INVESTMENT GOALS

- [ ] _____
- [ ] _____
- [ ] _____

TITHE TRACKER

Month: _____

DATE	TITHE AMOUNT	GIVEN TO:	NOTE/ SCRIPTURE

"Bring all the tithes into the storehouse..." — Malachi 3:10 (NLT)

MONTHLY FINANCIAL GOALS

What big goaI do I want to accomplish this month (Big Picture)?

TITHING GOALS

- [ ] _____
- [ ] _____
- [ ] _____

BUSINESS SAVINGS GOALS

- [ ] _____
- [ ] _____
- [ ] _____

PERSONAL SAVINGS GOALS

- [ ] _____
- [ ] _____
- [ ] _____

INVESTMENT GOALS

- [ ] _____
- [ ] _____
- [ ] _____

TITHE TRACKER

Month: _____

DATE	TITHE AMOUNT	GIVEN TO:	NOTE/ SCRIPTURE

"Bring all the tithes into the storehouse..." — Malachi 3:10 (NLT)

MONTHLY FINANCIAL GOALS

What big goaI do I want to accomplish this month (Big Picture)?

TITHING GOALS

- [ ] _____
- [ ] _____
- [ ] _____

BUSINESS SAVINGS GOALS

- [ ] _____
- [ ] _____
- [ ] _____

PERSONAL SAVINGS GOALS

- [ ] _____
- [ ] _____
- [ ] _____

INVESTMENT GOALS

- [ ] _____
- [ ] _____
- [ ] _____

TITHE TRACKER

Month: _____

DATE	TITHE AMOUNT	GIVEN TO:	NOTE/ SCRIPTURE

"Bring all the tithes into the storehouse..." — Malachi 3:10 (NLT)

MONTHLY FINANCIAL GOALS

What big goaI do I want to accomplish this month (Big Picture)?

TITHING GOALS

- [ ] _____
- [ ] _____
- [ ] _____

BUSINESS SAVINGS GOALS

- [ ] _____
- [ ] _____
- [ ] _____

PERSONAL SAVINGS GOALS

- [ ] _____
- [ ] _____
- [ ] _____

INVESTMENT GOALS

- [ ] _____
- [ ] _____
- [ ] _____

TITHE TRACKER

Month: _____

DATE	TITHE AMOUNT	GIVEN TO:	NOTE/ SCRIPTURE

"Bring all the tithes into the storehouse..." — Malachi 3:10 (NLT)

MONTHLY FINANCIAL GOALS

What big goaI do I want to accomplish this month (Big Picture)?

TITHING GOALS

- [ ] _____
- [ ] _____
- [ ] _____

BUSINESS SAVINGS GOALS

- [ ] _____
- [ ] _____
- [ ] _____

PERSONAL SAVINGS GOALS

- [ ] _____
- [ ] _____
- [ ] _____

INVESTMENT GOALS

- [ ] _____
- [ ] _____
- [ ] _____

TITHE TRACKER

Month: _____

DATE	TITHE AMOUNT	GIVEN TO:	NOTE/ SCRIPTURE

"Bring all the tithes into the storehouse..." — Malachi 3:10 (NLT)

MONTHLY FINANCIAL GOALS

What big goaI do I want to accomplish this month (Big Picture)?

TITHING GOALS

- [ ] _____
- [ ] _____
- [ ] _____

BUSINESS SAVINGS GOALS

- [ ] _____
- [ ] _____
- [ ] _____

PERSONAL SAVINGS GOALS

- [ ] _____
- [ ] _____
- [ ] _____

INVESTMENT GOALS

- [ ] _____
- [ ] _____
- [ ] _____

TITHE TRACKER

Month: _____

DATE	TITHE AMOUNT	GIVEN TO:	NOTE/ SCRIPTURE

"Bring all the tithes into the storehouse..." — Malachi 3:10 (NLT)

SOCIAL
MEDIA
PLANNER

Daily Post Planner

MUST POST TODAY

- ☐
- ☐
- ☐
- ☐
- ☐

TO DO's

HASHTAGS/KEYWORDS

NOTES

Daily Post Planner

MUST POST TODAY

- [ ]
- [ ]
- [ ]
- [ ]
- [ ]

TO DO's

_____
_____
_____
_____
_____
_____
_____
_____
_____
_____
_____

HASHTAGS/KEYWORDS

_____
_____
_____
_____
_____
_____

NOTES

Daily Post Planner

MUST POST TODAY

- ☐
- ☐
- ☐
- ☐
- ☐

TO DO's

_____
_____
_____
_____
_____
_____
_____
_____
_____
_____

HASHTAGS/KEYWORDS

_____
_____
_____
_____
_____

NOTES

Daily Post Planner

MUST POST TODAY

- ☐
- ☐
- ☐
- ☐
- ☐

TO DO's

HASHTAGS/KEYWORDS

NOTES

Daily Post Planner

MUST POST TODAY

☐

☐

☐

☐

☐

TO DO's

HASHTAGS/KEYWORDS

NOTES

Daily Post Planner

MUST POST TODAY

- ☐
- ☐
- ☐
- ☐
- ☐

TO DO's

HASHTAGS/KEYWORDS

NOTES

Daily Post Planner

MUST POST TODAY

- [ ]
- [ ]
- [ ]
- [ ]
- [ ]

TO DO's

_____
_____
_____
_____
_____
_____
_____
_____
_____
_____

HASHTAGS/KEYWORDS

_____
_____
_____
_____
_____

NOTES

Daily Post Planner

MUST POST TODAY

- [ ]
- [ ]
- [ ]
- [ ]
- [ ]

TO DO's

_____
_____
_____
_____
_____
_____
_____
_____
_____
_____
_____

HASHTAGS/KEYWORDS

_____
_____
_____
_____
_____
_____

NOTES

Daily Post Planner

MUST POST TODAY

- [ ]
- [ ]
- [ ]
- [ ]
- [ ]

TO DO's

HASHTAGS/KEYWORDS

NOTES

Daily Post Planner

MUST POST TODAY

- [ ]
- [ ]
- [ ]
- [ ]
- [ ]

TO DO's

_____
_____
_____
_____
_____
_____
_____
_____
_____
_____

HASHTAGS/KEYWORDS

_____
_____
_____
_____
_____
_____

NOTES